W9-BAQ-715

First published in Great Britain by Brockhampton Press,
a member of the Hodder Headline Group,
20 Bloomsbury Street, London WC1B 3QA

ISBN 1 86019 303 X

Created and produced by Flame Tree Publishing,
part of The Foundry Creative Media Company Limited,
The Long House, Antrobus Road, Chiswick, London W4 5HY

Special thanks to
Kate Brown and Kelley Doak for their work on this series

Printed and bound in U.A.E.

Elizabeth Barrett Browning
A Burning Passion

Written and Compiled by
K. E. SULLIVAN

Contents

Introduction

*I love your verse with all my heart, dear Miss Barrett, – and this is no
off-hand complimentary letter that I shall write, – whatever else, no prompt
matter-of-course recognition of your genius, and there a graceful and natural
end of the thing.*
Robert Browning

Elizabeth Barrett was thirty-eight when Robert Browning wrote these words to her in 1845. They spawned a friendship which led to a correspondence of nearly six hundred letters and their secret marriage twenty months later. At the time, Elizabeth was a published and admired poet, her work natural, rapid and overflowing with emotion. She was described as both ethereal and hysterical; her considerably talented husband called her a genius, saying 'the true creative power is hers, not mine'. And Edmund Gosse, when placing Elizabeth in the context of English literature, spoke of, 'her hysterical violence, the Pythian vagueness and the Pythian shriek'. Whatever can be said of her poetic fashion, she was nonetheless a poet of extraordinary distinction, achieving celebrity which far outweighed that of her husband in their lifetime.

By the end of the nineteenth century, however, Elizabeth Barrett Browning's poems were dated. Her emotions, in the words of her biographer, Joanna Richardson, were 'too neurotic, too Victorian for the modern reader, her social and political judgements are flawed by her excessive passion.'

Elizabeth Barrett Browning was born on 6 March 1806, at Coxhoe Hall, Co. Durham. She was the eldest of twelve children (one of whom died in infancy), and born, she felt, for poetry. When Elizabeth was three the family moved to Hope End, in Herefordshire, and she wrote that her childhood there was, ' ... a lonely life, growing green as the grass round

it'. She had an affectionate relationship with her siblings, in particular, her brother Edward – 'Bro' – who was two years her junior, and she spent many long hours in his company. She had an equal dedication to poetry, which became a passion and an overwhelming focus of her young life. She wrote later, 'I used to make up rhymes over my bread and milk when I was nearly a baby.'

As a woman in the Victorian age, Elizabeth was not formally educated, but was a voracious reader and energetic seeker of knowledge. She read and studied an enormous breadth of subjects during her childhood, and sat in on Edward's lessons, thereby learning Greek, which she grew to love. She wrote *The Battle of Marathon*, in the spirit of Pope's *Iliad*, while only thirteen, and her comprehension was far beyond her years. Elizabeth's father arranged its publication, and six years later, she published 'An Essay on Mind', along with some other verse. In 1921, when Elizabeth was fifteen, she suffered an accident which caused damage to her spine and rendered her something of an invalid. Her boundless enthusiasm for life was quietened by this development, but she was purged by her great love of poetry and she was able to express her heartfelt passions through the written word. She read, wrote, studied and conversed constantly; self-educated and self-absorbed, she gleamed with emotion and enthusiasm.

Elizabeth's mother died when she was twenty-two, and her father ruled his large household with an iron will and an inflexible spirit. The girls were fiercely guarded; indeed, the idea of them forming relationships and marrying was to him an iniquity beyond the scope of his imagination. In 1832, the Barrett family moved to Devon, and then, in 1835, to London. It was 1838 when they settled at Wimpole Street, and it was the same year in which Elizabeth published *The Seraphim, and Other Poems*, and was struck down by an undiagnosed illness of the lungs. In order to recuperate, she was sent to Torquay with her brother Edward, where in 1840 he drowned. This sent his sister into paroxysms of guilt and grief which invalided her for life. She was never able to speak of the tragedy, and she resigned herself to a life of isolation and invalidism, a condition which was only altered when she met the poet Robert Browning.

Elizabeth laid on her sofa each day, never leaving her room, seeing few outside her immediate family. But there, in her lonely room, Elizabeth wrote and studied fervently, engaging in copious correspondence with some of the foremost writers and scholars of her day; she wrote book reviews and critiques, and contributed to journals and books on various subjects. Her widely based talents were appreciated, and she became a figure of some acclaim in the literary world. She published *Poems*, in 1844, and then engaged herself in a love affair which was perhaps the most romantic of all time.

Robert Browning was several years younger than Elizabeth. His first letter to her was full of enthusiasm and praise for Elizabeth and her work; he said, 'I do, as I say, love these books with all my heart – and I love you, too.' Elizabeth was enchanted by the praise, for she was an admirer of Browning, and their correspondence quickly became intimate, comprising some of the most exquisite love letters in literary history. The two poets were kindred spirits, spiritual lovers who had not even set eyes upon each other. When they finally did meet, Browning was smitten, wildly enchanted. He wrote, 'I am proud and happy in your friendship – now and ever.' Letters flew between them, culminating in an elopement in September 1846. Before their marriage, Elizabeth wrote to him, 'Dearest, I write one word, and have one will which is yours ...'.

Their marriage remained a secret from her family, to whom she returned briefly after the service. Six days later she left with Browning for Italy, where they lived in happiness for fifteen years. Elizabeth was transformed by her marriage;

Browning convinced her that her illness was imaginary, and she travelled avidly with her husband. She was able, in 1848 to conceive a child, Robert Wiedemann Barrett Browning, born on 9 March 1849, and later known as Penini or, perhaps more appropriately, Pen. Elizabeth's father refused to acknowledge her marriage, and cut off all ties.

Sonnets from the Portuguese, her eloquent and widely quoted love poems, were written while she was courting Browning, and published three years later, and her fame back in England was soaring; there was some talk, upon the death of Wordsworth, that she should be made Poet Laureate as his successor. But Elizabeth remained in Florence, earnestly adopting the role of mother, and 'caught up [in] their parental pleasure with a sort of passion'. However, Elizabeth suffered several miscarriages, and her health teetered dangerously; a short spell in London was followed by a return to Italy, where she was revived by the weather and cod-liver oil. The Brownings travelled back and forth between Florence and England, until, in 1856, they left England forever. Pen was to remain an only child and he was cosseted, 'kept in girlish clothes; his golden curls were brushed like a girl's.'

Elizabeth had been working on *Aurora Leigh* for many years, and in 1856 it was published at last, and three editions were brought out in a month. *Aurora Leigh*, a poetical romance, was greeted with great excitement; W. M. Rossetti wrote of it, 'I have read as yet something less than two books of it, stuffed and loaded with poetic beauty and passionate sympathy and insight ...' Virginia Woolf said that *Aurora Leigh* 'vividly communicated' what it felt like to be a Victorian.

Elizabeth was an emotional intellectual; her work brims with spirited discourse on politics, religion, love, and the plight of women. In 1860 a volume of her political verse, *Poems Before Congress*, was published, but was greeted with critical discouragement. Alethea Hayter wrote that Elizabeth, 'grew out of many of the formulas of her Congregationalist upbringing, but the emotional violence and terror of Evangelical expression had sunk into her mind.' Elizabeth herself wrote, 'the louder grows the battle, the quicker beats the drum in my heart. Never did a year of youth pass to me in a hotter fire and passion than the last was.' She called her life both 'full' and 'frail', and although her great spirit surged onwards, her body was weak.

The death, in 1860, of her sister Henrietta, to whom she had always remained close 'prostrated' her, and her father's death a few years earlier still clung to her conscience. The political situation in Italy thrust her deeper in despair, causing her to write, 'I can scarcely command voice or hand ...'. She died on 29 June 1861, in her husband's arms. He wrote afterwards, 'God took her to Himself as you would lift a sleeping child from a dark, uneasy bed into your arms and the light.'

Robert Browning's own literary star began to rise after her death, and he returned to England with Pen to become, with Tennyson, the leading English poet of his time.

Author's Note

Elizabeth Barrett Browning spent the most part of her life as an invalid, but her fierce and burning quest for knowledge fed her extraordinary intellect, and filled her verse with passion. There is a broad range of themes within her work, which reflected the breadth of her interests and obsessions. She wrote of love and religion, politics and spiritual attachments; she poured out her deepest feelings in her work, in perceptive and memorable verse, peppered with classical references, intense literary allusions. The following is a selection of her finest verse, chosen from across her career and characterized by its unremitting power and integrity.

Chronology

1806   Born in Coxhoe Hall, Co. Durham, on 6 March.

1809   Barrett family moves to Hope End in Herefordshire.

1817   Studies Greek and Latin with her brother Edward (Bro).

1820   *The Battle of Marathon* published by her father.

1821   Suffers illness which affects her spinal cord.

1826   Publishes *An Essay on Mind, with Other Poems,* anonymously.

1832   Family moves to Devonshire.

1835   *Prometheus Bound: Translated from the Greek of Aeschylus, and Miscellaneous Poems* published anonymously.

1835   Family moves to London.

1838   *The Seraphim and Other Poems* published. Sent to Torquay to convalesce.

1840   Bro drowns; Elizabeth becomes very ill.

1841   Acquires Flush, a golden cocker spaniel, who becomes her constant companion.

1844   *Poems* published.

1845   Begins correspondence with Robert Browning, and they meet in May of that year.

1846   Marries Robert Browning. They leave for Italy.

1847   Moves from Pisa to Florence; suffers miscarriage.

1848   Casa Guidi becomes their permanent home.

1849   Robert Wiedemann Barrett Browning (Pen) born.

1850   New edition of *Poems* published, including *Sonnets from the Portuguese.*

1851   *Casa Guidi Windows: A Poem* published.

1853   Begins *Aurora Leigh.*

1854   Flush dies.

1855   Suffers relapse of illness.

1856	Finishes *Aurora Leigh*, published in London. Legacy of a family friend makes the Brownings financially secure.
1860	*Poems Before Congress* published.
1861	Very ill in Rome; dies on 29 June; buried in Protestant Cemetery in Florence.
1862	*Last Poems* published.

Stanzas on the Death of Lord Byron

I am not now
That which I have been. – Childe Harold.

HE *was*, and *is* not! Graecia's trembling shore,
Sighing through all her palmy groves, shall tell
That Harold's pilgrimage at last is o'er –
Mute the impassioned tongue, and tuneful shell,
That erst was wont in noblest strains to swell –
Hushed the proud shouts that rode Aegaea's wave!
For lo! the great Deliv'rer breathes farewell!
Gives to the world his mem'ry and a grave –
Expiring in the land he only lived to save!

Mourn, Hellas, mourn! and o'er thy widowed brow,
For ay, the cypress wreath of sorrow twine;
And in thy new-formed beauty, desolate, throw
The fresh-culled flowers on *his* sepulchral shrine.
Yes! let that heart whose fervour was all thine,
In consecrated urn lamented be!
That generous heart where genius thrilled divine,
Hath spent its last most glorious throb for thee –
Then sank amid the storm that made thy children free!

Britannia's poet! Graecia's hero, sleeps!
And Freedom, bending o'er the breathless clay,
Lifts up her voice, and in her anguish weeps!
For *us*, a night hath clouded o'er our day,
And hushed the lips that breathed our fairest lay.
Alas! and must the British lyre resound
A requiem, while the spirit wings away
Of him who on its strings such music found,
And taught its startling chords to give so sweet a sound!

The theme grows sadder – but my soul shall find
A language in these tears! No more – no more!
Soon, 'midst the shriekings of the tossing wind,
The 'dark blue depths' he sang of, shall have bore
 Our *all* of Byron to his native shore!
 His grave is thick with voices – to the ear
 Murm'ring an awful tale of greatness o'er;
But Memory strives with Death, and lingering near,
Shall consecrate the dust of Harold's lonely bier!

To —

MINE IS a wayward lay;
And, if its echoing rimes I try to string
Proveth a truant thing,
Whenso some names I love, send it away!

For then, eyes swimming o'er,
And clapsèd hands, and smiles in fondness meant,
Are much more eloquent –
So it had fain begone, and speak no more!

Yet it shall come again,
Ah, friend beloved! if so thy wishes be,
And, with wild melody,
I will, upon thine ear, cadence my strain –

Cadence my simple line,
Unfashioned by the cunning hand of Art,
But coming from my heart,
To tell the message of its love to thine!

As ocean shells, when taken
From Ocean's bed, will faithfully repeat
Her ancient music sweet –
Ev'n so these words, true to my heart, shall waken!

Oh! while our bark is seen,
Our little bark of kindly, social love,
Down life's clear stream to move
Toward the summer shores, where all is green –

So long thy name shall bring
Echoes of joy unto the grateful gales,
And thousand tender tales,
To freshen the fond hearts that round thee cling!

Hast thou not looked upon
The flowerets of the field in lowly dress?
Blame not my simpleness –
Think only of my love! – my song is gone.

The Autumn

GO, SIT upon the lofty hill,
And turn your eyes around,
Where waving woods and waters wild
Do hymn an autumn sound.
The summer sun is faint on them –
The summer flowers depart –
Sit still – as all transformed to stone,
Except your musing heart.

How there you sate in summer-time,
May yet be in your mind;
And how you heard the green woods sing
Beneath the freshening wind.
Though the same wind now blows around,
You would its blast recall;
For every breath that stirs the trees
Doth cause a leaf to fall.

Oh! like that wind, is all the mirth
That flesh and dust impart;
We cannot bear its visitings,
When change is on the heart.
Gay words and jests may make us smile
When Sorrow is asleep;
But other things must make us smile
When Sorrow bids us *weep*!

The dearest hands that clasp our hands, –
Their presence may be o'er;
The dearest voice that meets our ear,
That tone may come no more!
Youth fades; and then, the joys of youth,
Which once refreshed our mind,
Shall come – as, on those sighing woods,
The chilling autumn wind.

Hear not the wind – view not the woods;
Look out o'er vale and hill:
In spring, the sky encircled them –
The sky is round them still.
Come autumn's scathe, come winter's cold,
Come change – and human fate!
Whatever prospect HEAVEN doth bound
Can ne'er be desolate.

To Victoire, On Her Marriage

VICTOIRE! I knew thee in thy land,
Where I was strange to all:
I heard thee; and were strange to me
The words thy lips let fall.

I loved thee – for the Babel curse
Was meant not for the heart:
I parted from thee, in such way
As those who love may part.

And now a change hath come to us,
A sea doth rush between!
I do not know if we can be
Again as we have been.

I sit down in mine English land,
Mine English hearth beside;
And thou, to one I never knew,
Art plighted for a bride.

It will not wrong thy present joy
With bygone days to wend;
Nor wrongeth it mine English hearth
To love my Gallic friend.

Bind, bind the wreath! the slender ring
Thy wedded finger press!
May he who calls thy love his own,
Call so thine happiness!

Be he Terpander to thine heart,
And string fresh strings of gold,
Which may outgive new melodies,
But never mar the old!

And though I clasp no more thy hand
In my hand, and rejoice –
And though I see thy face no more,
And hear no more thy voice –

Farewell, farewell! – let thought of me
Visit thine heart! There is
In mine the very selfish prayer
That prayeth for thy bliss!

Weariness

MINE EYES are weary of surveying
The fairest things, too soon decaying;
Mine ears are weary of receiving
The kindest words – ah, past believing!
Weary my hope, of ebb and flow;
Weary my pulse, of tunes of woe:
My trusting heart is weariest!
I would – I would I were at rest!

For me, can earth refuse to fade?
For me, can words be faithful made?
Will my embittered hope be sweet?
My pulse forgo the human beat?
No! Darkness must consume mine eye –
Silence, mine ear – hope cease – pulse die –
And o'er mine heart a stone be pressed –
Or vain this, – 'Would I were at rest!'

There is a land of rest deferred:
Nor eye hath seen, nor ear hath heard,
Nor Hope hath trod the precinct o'er;
For hope beheld is hope no more!
There, human pulse forgets its tone –
There, hearts may know as they are known!
Oh, for dove's wings, thou dwelling blest,
To fly to thee, and be at rest!

Remonstrance

OH, SAY not it is vain to weep
That deafened bier above;
Where genius has made room for death,
And life is past from love;
That tears can never his bright looks
And tender words restore:
I know it is most vain to weep –
And therefore weep the more!

Oh, say not I shall cease to weep
When years have withered by;
That ever I shall speak of joy,
As if he could reply;
That ever mine unquivering lips
Shall name the name he bore:
I know that I may cease to weep,
And therefore weep the more!

Say, Time, who slew mine happiness,
Will leave to me my woe;
And woe's own stony strength shall chain
These tears' impassioned flow:
Or say, that these, my ceaseless tears,
May life to death restore;
For then my soul were wept away,
And I should weep no more!

REPLY

To weep awhile beside the bier,
Whereon his ashes lie,
Is well! — I know that rains must fall
When clouds are in the sky:
I know, *to die — to part*, will cloud
The brightest spirit o'er;
And yet, wouldst *thou* for ever weep,
When *he* can weep no more?

Fix not thy sight so long and fast
Upon the shroud's despair;
Look upward unto Zion's hill,
For death was also *there*!
And think, 'The death, the scourge, the scorn,
My sinless Saviour bore —
The curse — the pang, too deep for tears —
That I should weep no more!'

The Cry of the Children

I

DO YE hear the children weeping, O my brothers,
Ere the sorrow comes with years?
They are leaning their young heads against their mothers,
And *that* cannot stop their tears.
The young lambs are bleating in the meadows,
The young birds are chirping in the nest,
The young fawns are playing with the shadows,
The young flowers are blowing toward the west –
But the young, young children, O my brothers,
They are weeping bitterly!
They are weeping in the playtime of the others,
In the country of the free.

II

Do you question the young children in the sorrow,
Why their tears are falling so?
The old man may weep for his to-morrow
Which is lost in Long Ago;
The old tree is leafless in the forest
The old year is ending in the frost,
The old wound, if stricken, is the sorest,
The old hope is hardest to be lost.
But the young, young children, O my brothers,
Do you ask them why they stand
Weeping sore before the bosoms of their mothers,
In our happy Fatherland?

III

They look up with their pale and sunken faces,
And their looks are sad to see,
For the man's hoary anguish draws and presses
Down the cheeks of infancy.
'Your old earth,' they say, 'is very dreary;
Our young feet,' they say, 'are very weak!
Few paces have we taken, yet are weary –
Our grave-rest is very far to seek.
Ask the aged why they weep, and not the children;
For the outside earth is cold;
And we young ones stand without, in our bewildering,
And the graves are for the old.'

IV

'True,' say the children, 'it may happen
That we die before our time;
Little Alice died last year – her grave is shapen
Like a snowball, in the rime.
We looked into the pit prepared to take her:
Was no room for any work in the close clay!
From the sleep wherein she lieth none will wake her,
Crying, "Get up, little Alice! it is day."
If you listen by that grave, in sun and shower,
With your ear down, little Alice never cries;
Could we see her face, be sure we should not know her,
For the smile has time for growing in her eyes:
And merry go her moments, lulled and stilled in
The shroud by the kirk-chime!
It is good when it happens,' say the children,
'That we die before our time.'

V

Alas, alas, the children! they are seeking
Death in life, as best to have;
They are binding up their hearts away from breaking,
With a cerement from the grave.
Go out, children, from the mine and from the city,
Sing out, children, as the little thrushes do;
Pluck you handfuls of the meadow cowslips pretty,
Laugh aloud, to feel your fingers let them through!
But they answer, 'Are your cowslips of the meadows
Like our weeds anear the mine?
Leave us quiet in the dark of the coal-shadows,
From your pleasures fair and fine!

VI

'For oh,' say the children, 'we are weary,
And we cannot run or leap;
If we cared for any meadows, it were merely
To drop down in them and sleep.
Our knees tremble sorely in the stooping,
We fall upon our faces, trying to go;
And, underneath our heavy eyelids drooping,
The reddest flower would look as pale as snow;
For, all day, we drag our burden tiring
Through the coal-dark, underground –
Or, all day, we drive the wheels of iron
In the factories, round and round.

VII

'For, all day, the wheels are droning, turning,–
Their wind comes in our faces,–
Till our hearts turn, – our head, with pulses burning,
And the walls turn in their places:
Turns the sky in the high window blank and reeling,
Turns the long light that drops adown the wall,
Turn the black flies that crawl along the ceiling,
All are turning, all the day, and we with all.
And all day, the iron wheels are droning,
And sometimes we could pray,
"O ye wheels" (breaking out in a mad moaning),
"Stop! be silent for to-day!" '

VIII

Aye! be silent! Let them hear each other breathing
For a moment, mouth to mouth!
Let them touch each other's hands, in a fresh wreathing
Of their tender human youth!
Let them feel that this cold metallic motion
Is not all the life God fashions or reveals:
Let them prove their living souls against the notion
That they live in you, or under you, O wheels! –
Still, all day, the iron wheels go onward,
Grinding life down from its mark;
And the children's souls, which God is calling sunward,
Spin on blindly in the dark.

IX

Now tell the poor young children, O my brothers,
To look up to Him and pray;
So the blessèd One who blesseth all the others,
Will bless them another day.
They answer, 'Who is God that He should hear us,
While the rushing of the iron wheels is stirred?
When we sob aloud, the human creatures near us
Pass by, hearing not, or answer not a word.
And *we* hear not (for the wheels in their resounding)
Strangers speaking at the door:
Is it likely God, with angels singing round Him,
Hears our weeping any more?

X

'Two words, indeed, of praying we remember,
And at midnight's hour of harm,
"Our Father," looking upward in the chamber,
We say softly for a charm.
We know no other words, except "Our Father,"
And we think that, in some pause of angels' song,
God may pluck them with the silence sweet to gather,
And hold both within His right hand which is strong.
"Our Father!" If He heard us, He would surely
(For they call Him good and mild)
Answer, smiling down the steep world very purely,
"Come and rest with Me, My child."

XI

'But, no!' say the children, weeping faster,
　'He is speechless as a stone;
And they tell us, of His image is the master
　Who commands us to work on.
Go to!' say the children, – 'up in Heaven,
Dark, wheel-like, turning clouds are all we find.
Do not mock us; grief has made us unbelieving –
We look up for God, but tears have made us blind.'
Do you hear the children weeping and disproving
　O my brothers, what ye preach?
For God's possible is taught by His world's loving,
　And the children doubt of each.

XII

And well may the children weep before you!
　They are weary ere they run;
They have never seen the sunshine, nor the glory
　Which is brighter than the sun.
They know the grief of man, without its wisdom;
　They sink in man's despair, without its calm;
Are slaves, without the liberty in Christdom,
　Are martyrs, by the pang without the palm, –
Are worn, as if with age, yet unretrievingly
　The harvest of its memories cannot reap, –
Are orphans of the earthly love and heavenly.
　Let them weep! let them weep!

XIII

They look up, with their pale and sunken faces,
  And their look is dread to see,
For they mind you of their angels in high places,
  With eyes turned on Deity! –
'How long,' they say, 'how long, O cruel nation,
Will you stand, to move the world, on a child's heart, –
Stifle down with a mailed heel its palpitation,
And tread onward to your throne amid the mart?
  Our blood splashes upward, O gold-heaper,
  And your purple shows your path!
But the child's sob in the silence curses deeper
  Than the strong man in his wrath.'

Sleeping and Watching

I

SLEEP ON, baby, on the floor,
Tired of all the playing!
Sleep with smile the sweeter for
That, you dropped away in!
On your curls' full roundness, stand
Golden lights serenely;
One cheek, pushed out by the hand,
Folds the dimple inly.
Little head and little foot
Heavy laid for pleasure,
Underneath the lids half shut,
Slants the shining azure. –
Open-soul in noonday sun,
So, you lie and slumber!
Nothing evil having done,
Nothing can encumber.

II

I, who cannot sleep as well,
Shall I sigh to view you?
Or sigh further to foretell
All that may undo you?
Nay, keep smiling, little child,
Ere the sorrow neareth:
I will smile too! patience mild
Pleasure's token weareth.
Nay, keep sleeping before loss:
I shall sleep though losing!
As by cradle, so by cross,
Sure is the reposing.

III

And God knows who sees us twain,
Child at childish leisure,
I am near as tired of pain
As you seem of pleasure.
Very soon too, by His grace
Gently wrapt around me,
Shall I show as calm a face,
Shall I sleep as soundly.
Differing in this, that you
Clasp your playthings, sleeping,
While my hand shall drop the few
Given to my keeping:
Differing in this, that I
Sleeping shall be colder,
And in waking presently,
Brighter to beholder:
Differing in this beside
(Sleeper, have you heard me?
Do you move, and open wide
Eyes of wonder toward me?) —
That while you, I thus recall
From your sleep, I solely,
Me from mine an angel shall,
With reveillie holy.

A Child's Thought of God

I

THEY SAY that God lives very high:
But if you look above the pines
You cannot see our God; and why?

II

And if you dig down in the mines
You never see Him in the gold;
Though, from Him, all that's glory shines.

III

God is so good, He wears a fold
Of heaven and earth across His face –
Like secrets kept, for love, untold.

IV

But still I feel that His embrace
Slides down by thrills, through all things made,
Through sight and sound of every place.

V

As if my tender mother laid
On my shut lids her kisses' pressure,
Half-waking me at night, and said
'Who kissed you through the dark, dear guesser?'

The Sleep

He giveth His beloved sleep. — Ps. cxxvii. 2.

I

OF ALL the thoughts of God that are
Borne inward unto souls afar,
Along the Psalmist's music deep,
Now tell me if that any is,
For gift or grace, surpassing this —
'He giveth His belovèd, sleep?'

II

What would we give to our beloved?
The hero's heart, to be unmoved,
The poet's star-tuned harp, to sweep,
The patriot's voice, to teach and rouse,
The monarch's crown, to light the brows? —
He giveth His belovèd, sleep.

III

What do we give to our beloved?
A little faith all undisproved,
A little dust to overweep,
And bitter memories to make
The whole earth blasted for our sake.
He giveth His belovèd, sleep.

IV

'Sleep soft, beloved!' we sometimes say,
But have no tune to charm away
Sad dreams that through the eyelids creep.
But never doleful dream again
Shall break the happy slumber when
He giveth His belovèd, sleep.

V

O earth, so full of dreary noises!
O men, with wailing in your voices!
O delvèd gold, the wailers heap!
O strife, O curse, that o'er it fall!
God strikes a silence through you all,
And giveth His belovèd, sleep.

VI

His dews drop mutely on the hill;
His cloud above it saileth still,
Though on its slope men sow and reap.
More softly than the dew is shed,
Or cloud is floated overhead,
He giveth His belovèd, sleep.

VII

Aye, men may wonder while they scan
A living, thinking, feeling man
Confirmed in such a rest to keep;
But angels say, and through the word
I think their happy smile is *heard* —
'He giveth His belovèd, sleep.'

VIII

For me, my heart that erst did go
Most like a tired child at a show,
That sees through tears the mummers leap,
Would now its wearied vision close,
Would childlike on His love repose,
Who giveth His belovèd, sleep.

IX

And, friends, dear friends, – when it shall be
That this low breath is gone from me,
And round my bier ye come to weep,
Let One, most loving of you all,
Say, 'Not a tear must o'er her fall;
He giveth His belovèd, sleep.'

Tears

THANK GOD, bless God, all ye who suffer not
More grief than ye can weep for. That is well —
That is light grieving! lighter, none befell
Since Adam forfeited the primal lot.
Tears! what are tears? The babe weeps in its cot,
The mother singing, — at her marriage-bell
The bride weeps, — and before the oracle
Of high-faned hills, the poet has forgot
Such moisture on his cheeks. Thank God for grace,
Ye who weep only! If, as some have done,
Ye grope tear-blinded in a desert place
And touch but tombs, — look up! those tears will run
Soon in long rivers down the lifted face,
And leave the vision clear for stars and sun.

Grief

I TELL YOU, hopeless grief is passionless;
That only men incredulous of despair,
Half-taught in anguish, through the midnight air
Beat upward to God's throne in loud access
Of shrieking and reproach. Full desertness
In souls, as countries, lieth silent-bare
Under the blanching, vertical eye-glare
Of the absolute Heavens. Deep-hearted man, express
Grief for thy Dead in silence like to death: –
Most like a monumental statue set
In everlasting watch and moveless woe,
Till itself crumble to the dust beneath.
Touch it: the marble eyelids are not wet;
If it could weep, it could arise and go.

A Thought for a Lonely Death-Bed

INSCRIBED TO MY FRIEND E.C.

IF GOD compel thee to this destiny,
To die alone, – with none beside thy bed
To ruffle round with sobs thy last word said,
And mark with tears the pulses ebb from thee, –
Pray then alone – 'O Christ, come tenderly!
By Thy forsaken Sonship in the red
Drear wine-press, – by the wilderness outspread, –
And the lone garden where Thine agony
Fell bloody from Thy brow, – by all of those
Permitted desolations, comfort mine!
No earthly friend being near me, interpose
No deathly angel 'twixt my face and Thine,
But stoop Thyself to gather my life's rose,
And smile away my mortal to Divine.'

Pain in Pleasure

A THOUGHT lay like a flower upon mine heart,
And drew around it other thoughts like bees
For multitude and thirst of sweetnesses, –
Whereat rejoicing, I desired the art
Of the Greek whistler, who to wharf and mart
Could lure those insect swarms from orange-trees,
That I might hive with me such thoughts, and please
My soul so, always. Foolish counterpart
Of a weak man's vain wishes! While I spoke,
The thought I called a flower, grew nettle-rough –
The thoughts, called bees, stung me to festering.
Oh, entertain (cried Reason, as she woke)
Your best and gladdest thoughts but long enough,
And they will all prove sad enough to sting.

Discontent

LIGHT HUMAN nature is too lightly tost
And ruffled without cause, – complaining on, –
Restless with rest – until, being overthrown,
It learneth to lie quiet. Let a frost
Or a small wasp have crept to the innermost
Of our ripe peach, or let the wilful sun
Shine westward of our window, – straight we run
A furlong's sigh, as if the world were lost.
But what time through the heart and through the brain
God hath transfixed us, – we, so moved before,
Attain to a calm. Aye, shouldering weights of pain,
We anchor in deep waters, safe from shore,
And hear, submissive, o'er the stormy main,
God's chartered judgements walk for evermore.

Life

EACH CREATURE holds an insular point in space;
Yet what man stirs a finger, breathes a sound,
But all the multitudinous beings round
In all the countless worlds, with time and place
For their conditions, down to the central base,
Thrill, haply, in vibration and rebound,
Life answering life across the vast profound,
In full antiphony, by a common grace?
I think, this sudden joyaunce which illumes
A child's mouth sleeping, unaware may run
From some soul newly loosened from earth's tombs.
I think, this passionate sigh, which half-begun
I stifle back, may reach and stir the plumes
Of God's calm angel standing in the sun.

Love

WE CANNOT live, except thus mutually
We alternate, aware or unaware,
The reflex act of life; and when we bear
Our virtue outward most impulsively,
Most full of invocation, and to be
Most instantly compellant, certes, there
We live most life, whoever breathes most air,
And counts his dying years by sun and sea.
But when a soul, by choice and conscience, doth
Throw out her full force on another soul,
The conscience and the concentration both
Make mere life, Love. For Life in perfect whole
And aim consummated, is love in sooth,
As nature's magnet-heat rounds pole with pole.

Cowper's Grave

I

IT IS a place where poets crowned may feel
    the heart's decaying;
It is a place where happy saints may weep
    amid their praying.
Yet let the grief and humbleness, as low
    as silence, languish:
Earth surely now may give her calm to whom
    she gave her anguish.

II

O poets, from a maniac's tongue was poured
    the deathless singing!
O Christians, at your cross of hope, a hopeless
    hand was clinging!
O men, this man in brotherhood your
    weary paths beguiling,
Groaned inly while he taught you peace, and died
    while ye were smiling!

III

And now, what time ye all may read through
    dimming tears his story,
How discord on the music fell, and
    darkness on the glory,
And how when, one by one, sweet sounds and
    wandering lights departed,
He wore no less a loving face because
    so broken-hearted,

IV

He shall be strong to sanctify the
poet's high vocation,
And bow the meekest Christian down
in meeker adoration;
Nor ever shall he be, in praise, by wise
or good forsaken,
Named softly as the household name of one
whom God hath taken.

V

With quiet sadness and no gloom I learn
to think upon him, –
With meekness that is gratefulness to God whose
heaven hath won him,
Who suffered once the madness-cloud to His
own love to blind him,
But gently led the blind along where breath and
bird could find him;

VI

And wrought within his shattered brain such
quick poetic senses
As hills have language for, and stars,
harmonious influences.
The pulse of dew upon the grass, kept his
within its number,
And silent shadows from the trees refreshed
him like a slumber.

VII

Wild timid hares were drawn from woods to
share his home-caresses,
Uplooking to his human eyes with
sylvan tendernesses.
The very world, by God's constraint, from
falsehood's ways removing,
Its women and its men became, beside him,
true and loving.

VIII

And though, in blindness, he remained
unconscious of that guiding,
And things provided came without the sweet
sense of providing,
He testified this solemn truth, while
frenzy desolated,
– Nor man nor nature satisfy whom
only God created.

IX

Like a sick child that knoweth not his mother
while she blesses
And drops upon his burning brow the
coolness of her kisses, –
That turns his fevered eyes around – 'My mother!
where's my mother?' –
As if such tender words and deeds could
come from any other! –

X

The fever gone, with leaps of heart he sees her
bending o'er him,
Her face all pale from watchful love, the unweary
love she bore him! –
Thus, woke the poet from the dream his life's
long fever gave him,
Beneath those deep pathetic Eyes, which closed
in death to save him.

XI

Thus? oh not thus! no type of earth can
image that awaking,
Wherein he scarcely heard the chant of seraphs,
round him breaking,
Or felt the new immortal throb of soul
from body parted,
But felt those eyes alone, and knew, –
'My Saviour! not deserted!'

XII

Deserted! Who hath dreamt that when the
cross in darkness rested,
Upon the Victim's hidden face, no
love was manifested?
What frantic hands outstretched have
e'er the atoning drops averted?
What tears have washed them from the soul,
that one should be deserted?

XIII

Deserted! God could separate from
His own essence rather;
And Adam's sins *have* swept between the
righteous Son and Father.
Yea, once, Immanuel's orphaned cry
His universe hath shaken –
It went up single, echoless,
'My God, I am forsaken!'

XIV

It went up from the Holy's lips
amid His lost creation,
That, of the lost, no son should use those
words of desolation!
That earth's worst frenzies, marring hope, should
mar not hope's fruition,
And I, on Cowper's grave, should see
his rapture in a vision.

Song of the Rose

ATTRIBUTED TO SAPPHO

IF ZEUS chose us a King of the flowers in his mirth,
He would call to the rose and would royally crown it,
For the rose, ho, the rose! is the grace of the earth,
Is the light of the plants that are growing upon it.
For the rose, ho, the rose! is the eye of the flowers,
Is the blush of the meadows that feel themselves fair, –
Is the lightning of beauty, that strikes through the bowers
On pale lovers who sit in the glow unaware.
Ho, the rose breathes of love! ho, the rose lifts the cup
To the red lips of Cypris invoked for a guest!
Ho, the rose, having curled its sweet eaves for the world,
Takes delight in the motion its petals keep up,
As they laugh to the Wind as it laughs from the west.

Sonnets From The Portuguese
EXTRACTS

I

I THOUGHT once how Theocritus had sung
Of the sweet years, the dear and wished-for years,
Who each one in a gracious hand appears
To bear a gift for mortals, old or young:
And, as I mused it in his antique tongue,
I saw, in gradual vision through my tears,
The sweet, sad years, the melancholy years,
Those of my own life, who by turns had flung
A shadow across me. Straightway I was 'ware,
So weeping, how a mystic Shape did move
Behind me, and drew me backward by the hair,
And a voice said in mastery while I strove, . .
'Guess now who holds thee?' – 'Death,' I said. But, there,
The silver answer rang, . . 'Not Death, but Love.'

III

UNLIKE are we, unlike, O princely Heart!
Unlike our uses and our destinies.
Our ministering two angels look surprise
On one another, as they strike athwart
Their wings in passing. Thou, bethink thee, art
A guest for queens to social pageantries,
With gages from a hundred brighter eyes
Than tears even can make mine, to ply thy part
Of chief musician. What hast thou to do
With looking from the lattice-lights at me,
A poor, tired, wandering singer, . . singing through
The dark, and leaning up a cypress tree?
The chrism is on thine head, – on mine, the dew, –
And Death must dig the level where these agree.

IV

THOU hast thy calling to some palace-floor,
Most gracious singer of high poems! where
The dancers will break footing, from the care
Of watching up thy pregnant lips for more.
And dost thou lift this house's latch too poor
For hand of thine? and canst thou think and bear
To let thy music drop here unaware
In folds of golden fullness at my door?
Look up and see the casement broken in,
The bats and owlets builders in the roof!
My cricket chirps against thy mandolin.
Hush, call no echo up in further proof
Of desolation! there's a voice within
That weeps . . . as thou must sing . . . alone, aloof.

VI

GO from me. Yet I feel that I shall stand
Henceforward in thy shadow. Nevermore
Alone upon the threshold of my door
Of individual life, I shall command
The uses of my soul, nor lift my hand
Serenely in the sunshine as before,
Without the sense of that which I forbore, . .
Thy touch upon the palm. The widest land
Doom takes to part us, leaves thy heart in mine
With pulses that beat double. What I do
And what I dream include thee, as the wine
Must taste of its own grapes. And when I sue
God for myself, He hears that name of thine,
And sees within my eyes the tears of two.

VIII

WHAT can I give thee back, O liberal
And princely giver, who hast brought the gold
And purple of thine heart, unstained, untold,
And laid them on the outside of the wall
For such as I take or leave withal,
In unexpected largesse? am I cold,
Ungrateful, that for these most manifold
High gifts, I render nothing back at all?
Not so; not cold, – but very poor instead.
Ask God who knows. For frequent tears have run
The colours from my life, and left so dead
And pale a stuff, it were not fitly done
To give the same as pillow to thy head.
Go farther! let it serve to trample on.

X

YET, love, mere love, is beautiful indeed
And worthy of acceptation. Fire is bright,
Let temple burn, or flax. An equal light
Leaps in the flame from cedar-plank or weed.
And love is fire; and when I say at need
I love thee .. mark! .. *I love thee!* .. in thy sight
I stand transfigured, glorified aright,
With conscience of the new rays that proceed
Out of my face toward thine. There's nothing low
In love, when love the lowest: meanest creatures
Who love God, God accepts while loving so.
And what I *feel*, across the inferior features
Of what I *am*, doth flash itself, and show
How that great work of Love enhances Nature's.

XIV

IF thou must love me, let it be for nought
Except for love's sake only. Do not say
'I love her for her smile . . . her look . . . her way
Of speaking gently, . . for a trick of thought
That falls in well with mine, and certes brought
A sense of pleasant ease on such a day' –
For these things in themselves, Belovèd, may
Be changed, or change for thee, – and love, so wrought,
May be unwrought so. Neither love me for
Thine own dear pity's wiping my cheeks dry, –
A creature might forget to weep, who bore
Thy comfort long, and lose thy love thereby!
But love me for love's sake, that evermore
Thou mayst love on, through love's eternity.

XXVIII

MY letters! all dead paper, . . mute and white! –
And yet they seem alive and quivering
Against my tremulous hands which loose the string
And let them drop down on my knee to-night.
This said, . . he wished to have me in his sight
Once, as a friend: this fixed a day in spring
To come and touch my hand . . . a simple thing,
Yet I wept for it! – this, . . the paper's light . . .
Said, *Dear, I love thee;* and I sank and quailed
As if God's future thundered on my past.
This said, *I am thine* – and so its ink has paled
With lying at my heart that beat too fast.
And this . . . O Love, thy words have ill availed,
If, what this said, I dared repeat at last!

XLIII

HOW do I love thee? Let me count the ways.
I love thee to the depth and breadth and height
My soul can reach, when feeling out of sight
For the ends of Being and ideal Grace.
I love thee to the level of every day's
Most quiet need, by sun and candlelight.
I love thee freely, as men strive for Right;
I love thee purely, as they turn from Praise.
I love thee with the passion put to use
In my old griefs, and with my childhood's faith.
I love thee with a love I seemed to lose
With my lost saints, – I love thee with the breath,
Smiles, tears, of all my life! – and, if God choose,
I shall but love thee better after death.

Bereavement

WHEN SOME Belovèds, 'neath whose eyelids lay
The sweet lights of my childhood, one by one
Did leave me dark before the natural sun,
And I astonished fell and could not pray, —
A thought within me to myself did say,
'Is God less God, that thou art left undone?
Rise, worship, bless Him, in this sack-cloth spun,
As in that purple!' — But I answered, Nay!
What child his filial heart in words can loose,
If he behold his tender father raise
The hand that chastens sorely? can he choose
But sob in silence with an upward gaze? —
And my great Father, thinking fit to bruise,
Discerns in speechless tears both prayer and praise.

Past and Future

MY FUTURE will not copy fair my past
On any leaf but Heaven's. Be fully done,
Supernal Will! I would not fain be one
Who, satisfying thirst and breaking fast
Upon the fullness of the heart, at last
Says no grace after meat. My wine has run
Indeed out of my cup, and there is none
To gather up the bread of my repast
Scattered and trampled, – yet I find some good
In earth's green herbs, and streams that bubble up
Clear from the darkling ground, – content until
I sit with angels before better food.
Dear Christ! when Thy new vintage fills my cup,
This hand shall shake no more, nor that wine spill.

Work

WHAT ARE we set on earth for? Say, to toil;
Nor seek to leave thy tending of the vines,
For all the heat o' the day, till it declines,
And Death's mild curfew shall from work assoil.
God did anoint thee with His odorous oil,

To wrestle, not to reign; and He assigns
All thy tears over, like pure crystallines,
For younger fellow workers of the soil
To wear for amulets. So others shall
Take patience, labour, to their heart, and hand,
From thy hand, and thy heart, and thy brave cheer,
And God's grace fructify through thee all.
The least flower, with a brimming cup, may stand,
And share its dewdrop with another near.

Casa Guidi Windows: A Poem

—————— EXTRACT ——————

I

I HEARD last night a little child go singing
’Neath Casa Guidi windows, by the church,
O bella libertà, O bella! stringing
The same words still on notes he went in search
So high for, you concluded the upspringing
Of such a nimble bird to sky from perch
Must leave the whole bush in a tremble green,
And that the heart of Italy must beat,
While such a voice had leave to rise serene
’Twixt church and palace of a Florence street!
A little child, too, who not long had been
By mother’s finger steadied on his feet.
And still *O bella Libertà* he sang.

Aurora Leigh
—— EXTRACT ——

FIRST BOOK

OF WRITING many books there is no end;
And I who have written much in prose and verse
For others' uses, will write now for mine, –
Will write my story for my better self
As when you paint your portrait for a friend,
Who keeps it in a drawer and looks at it
Long after he has ceased to love you, just
To hold together what he was and is.

I, writing thus, am still what men call young,
I have not so far left the coasts of life
To travel inland, that I cannot hear
That murmur of the outer Infinite
Which unweaned babies smile at in their sleep
When wondered at for smiling; not so far,
But still I catch my mother at her post
Beside the nursery-door, with finger up,
'Hush, hush – here's too much noise!'
                    while her sweet eyes
Leap forward, taking part against her word
In the child's riot. Still I sit and feel
My father's slow hand, when she had left us both,
Stroke out my childish curls across his knee,
And hear Assunta's daily jest (she knew
He liked it better than a better jest)
Inquire how many golden seudi went
To make such ringlets. O my father's hand,
Stroke heavily, heavily the poor hair down,
Draw, press the child's head closer to thy knee!
I'm still too young, too young, to sit alone.

Christmas Gifts

I

THE POPE on Christmas Day
Sits in St. Peter's chair;
But the peoples murmur and say,
'Our souls are sick and forlorn,
And who will show us where
Is the stable where Christ was born?'

II

The star is lost in the dark;
The manger is lost in the straw;
The Christ cries faintly . . hark! . .
Through bands that swaddle and strangle –
But the Pope in the chair of awe
Looks down the great quadrangle.

III

The magi kneel at his foot,
Kings of the east and west,
But, instead of the angels (mute
Is the 'Peace on earth' of their song),
The peoples, perplexed and opprest,
Are sighing, 'How long, how long?'

IV

And, instead of the kine, bewilder in
Shadow of aisle and dome,
The bear who tore up the children,
The fox who burnt up the corn,
And the wolf who suckled at Rome
Brothers to slay and to scorn.

V

Cardinals left and right of him,
Worshippers round and beneath,
The silver trumpets at sight of him
Thrill with a musical blast:
But the people say through their teeth,
'Trumpets? we wait for the Last!'

VI

He sits in the place of the Lord,
And asks for the gifts of the time;
Gold, for the haft of a sword,
To win back Romagna averse,
Incense, to sweeten a crime,
And myrrh, to embitter a curse.

VII

Then a king of the west said, 'Good! —
I bring thee the gifts of the time;
Red, for the patriot's blood,
Green, for the martyr's crown,
White, for the dew and the rime,
When the morning of God comes down.'

VIII

— O mystic tricolor bright!
The Pope's heart quailed like a man's:
The cardinals froze at the sight,
Bowing their tonsures hoary:
And the eyes in the peacock-fans
Winked at the alien glory.

IX

But the peoples exclaimed in hope,
'Now blessed be he who has brought
These gifts of the time to the Pope,
When our souls were sick and forlorn.
– And *here* is the star we sought,
To show us where Christ was born!'

A Curse for a Nation

———— EXTRACT ————

PROLOGUE

I HEARD an angel speak last night,
And he said, 'Write!
Write a Nation's curse for me,
And send it over the Western Sea.'

I faltered, taking up the word:
'Not so, my lord!
If curses must be, choose another
To send thy curse against my brother.'

Little Mattie

DEAD! Thirteen a month ago!
Short and narrow her life's walk;
Lover's love she could not know
Even by a dream or talk:
Too young to be glad of youth,
Missing honour, labour, rest
And the warmth of a babe's mouth
At the blossom of her breast.
Must you pity her for this
And for all the loss it is,
You, her mother, with wet face,
Having had all in your case?

ELIZABETH BARRETT BROWNING

II

Just so young but yesternight
Now she is as old as death.
Meek, obedient in your sight,
Gentle to a beck or breath
Only on last Monday! Yours,
Answering you like silver bells
Lightly touched! An hour matures:
You can teach her nothing else.
She has seen the mystery hid
Under Egypt's pyramid:
By those eyelids pale and close
Now she knows what Rhamses knows.

III

Cross her quiet hands, and smooth
Down her patient locks of silk,
Cold and passive as in truth
You your fingers in spilt milk
Drew along a marble floor;
But her lips you cannot wring
Into saying a word more,
'Yes,' or 'No,' or such a thing:
Though you call and beg and wreak
Half your soul out in a shriek,
She will lie there in default
And most innocent revolt.

IV

Aye, and if she spoke, may be
She would answer like the Son,
'What is now 'twixt thee and me?'
Dreadful answer! better none.
Yours on Monday, God's to-day!
Yours, your child, your blood, your heart,
Called . . you called her, did you say,
'Little Mattie' for your part?
Now already it sounds strange,
And you wonder, in this change,
What He calls His angel-creature,
Higher up than you can reach her.

V

'Twas a green and easy world
As she took it; room to play
(Though one's hair might get uncurled
At the far end of the day).
What she suffered she shook off
In the sunshine; what she sinned
She could pray on high enough
To keep safe above the wind.
If reproved by God or you,
'Twas to better her, she knew;
And if crossed, she gathered still
'Twas to cross out something ill.

VI

You, you had the right, you thought,
To survey her with sweet scorn,
Poor gay child, who had not caught
Yet the octave-stretch forlorn
Of your larger wisdom! Nay,
Now your places are changed so,
In that same superior way
She regards you dull and low
As you did herself exempt
From life's sorrows. Grand contempt
Of the spirits risen awhile,
Who look back with such a smile!

VII

There's the sting of't. That, I think,
Hurts the most a thousandfold!
To feel sudden, at a wink,
Some dear child we used to scold,
Praise, love both ways, kiss and tease,
Teach and tumble as our own,
All its curls about our knees,
Rise up suddenly full-grown.
Who could wonder such a sight
Made a woman mad outright?
Show me Michael with the sword
Rather than such angels, Lord!

My Kate

I

She was not as pretty as women I know,
And yet all your best made of sunshine and snow
Drop to shade, melt to nought in the long-trodden ways,
While she's still remembered on warm and cold days –
           My Kate.

II

Her air had a meaning, her movements a grace;
You turned from the fairest to gaze on her face:
And when you had once seen her forehead and mouth,
You saw as distinctly her soul and her truth –
           My Kate.

III

Such a blue inner light from her eyelids outbroke,
You looked at her silence and fancied she spoke:
When she did, so peculiar yet soft was the tone,
Though the loudest spoke also, you heard her alone –
           My Kate.

IV

I doubt if she said to you much that could act
As a thought or suggestion: she did not attract
In the sense of the brilliant or wise: I infer
'Twas her thinking of others, made you think of her –
           My Kate.

V

She never found fault with you, never implied
Your wrong by her right; and yet men at her side
Grew nobler, girls purer, as through the whole town
The children were gladder that pulled at her gown –
                    My Kate.

VI

None knelt at her feet confessed lovers in thrall;
They knelt more to God than they used, – that was all:
If you praised her as charming, some asked what you meant,
But the charm of her presence was felt when she went –
                    My Kate.

VII

The weak and the gentle, the ribald and rude,
She took as she found them, and did them all good;
It always was so with her – see what you have!
She has made the grass greener even here .. with her grave –
                    My Kate.

VIII

My dear one! – when thou wast alive with the rest,
I held thee the sweetest and loved thee the best:
And now thou art dead, shall I not take thy part
As thy smiles used to do for thyself, my sweet Heart –
                    My Kate?

My Heart and I

I

ENOUGH! we're tired, my heart and I.
We sit beside the headstone thus,
And wish that name were carved for us.
The moss reprints more tenderly
The hard types of the mason's knife,
As heaven's sweet life renews earth's life
With which we're tired, my heart and I.

II

You see we're tired, my heart and I.
We dealt with books, we trusted men,
And in our own blood drenched the pen,
As if such colours couldn't fly.
We walked too straight for fortune's end,
We loved too true to keep a friend;
At last we're tired, my heart and I.

III

How tired we feel, my heart and I!
We seem of no use in the world;
Our fancies hang grey and uncurled
About men's eyes indifferently;
Our voice which thrilled you so, will let
You sleep; our tears are only wet:
What do we here, my heart and I?

IV

So tired, so tired, my heart and I!
It was not thus in that old time
When Ralph sate with me 'neath the lime
To watch the sunset from the sky.
'Dear love, you're looking tired,' he said;
I, smiling at him, shook my head:
'Tis now we're tired, my heart and I.

V

So tired, so tired, my heart and I!
Though now none takes me on his arm
To fold me close and kiss me warm
Till each quick breath end in a sigh
Of happy languor. Now, alone,
We lean upon this graveyard stone,
Uncheered, unkissed, my heart and I.

VI

Tired out we are, my heart and I.
Suppose the world brought diadems
To tempt us, crusted with loose gems
Of powers and pleasures? Let it try.
We scarcely care to look at even
A pretty child, or God's blue heaven,
We feel so tired, my heart and I.

VII

Yet who complains? My heart and I?
In this abundant earth no doubt
Is little room for things worn out:
Disdain them, break them, throw them by.
And if before the days grew rough
We *once* were loved, used, – well enough,
I think, we've fared, my heart and I.

A Musical Instrument

I

WHAT WAS he doing, the great god Pan,
Down in the reeds by the river?
Spreading ruin and scattering ban,
Splashing and paddling with hoofs of a goat,
And breaking the golden lilies afloat
With the dragon-fly on the river.

II

He tore out a reed, the great god Pan,
From the deep cool bed of the river:
The limpid water turbidly ran,
And the broken lilies a-dying lay,
And the dragon-fly had fled away,
Ere he brought it out of the river.

III

High on the shore sate the great god Pan,
While turbidly flowed the river;
And hacked and hewed as a great god can,
With his hard bleak steel at the patient reed,
Till there was not a sign of a leaf indeed
To prove it fresh from the river.

IV

He cut it short, did the great god Pan
(How tall it stood in the river!),
Then drew the pith, like the heart of a man,
Steadily from the outside ring,
And notched the poor dry empty thing
In holes, as he sate by the river.

V

'This is the way,' laughed the great god Pan
(Laughed while he sate by the river),
'The only way, since gods began
To make sweet music, they could succeed.'
Then, dropping his mouth to a hole in the reed,
He blew in power by the river.

VI

Sweet, sweet, sweet, O Pan!
Piercing sweet by the river!
Blinding sweet, O great god Pan!
The sun on the hill forgot to die,
And the lilies revived, and the dragon-fly
Came back to dream on the river.

VII

Yet half a beast is the great god Pan,
To laugh as he sits by the river,
Making a poet out of a man:
The true gods sigh for the cost and pain, —
For the reed which grows nevermore again
As a reed with the reeds in the river.

Parting Lovers
—— EXTRACT ——

I

I LOVE thee, love thee, Giulio;
Some call me cold, and some demure;
And if thou hast ever guessed that so
I loved thee . . well, the proof was poor,
And no one could be sure.

II

Before thy song (with shifted rimes
To suit my name) did I undo
The Persian? If it stirred sometimes,
Thou hast not seen a hand push through
A foolish flower or two.

Mother and Poet

TURIN, AFTER NEWS FROM GAETA, 1861

—— EXTRACT ——

I

DEAD! One of them shot by the sea in the east,
And one of them shot in the west by the sea.
Dead! both my boys! When you sit at the feast
And are wanting a great song for Italy free,
Let none look at me!

II

Yet I was a poetess only last year,
And good at my art, for a woman, men said;
But this woman, this, who is agonized here,
—The east sea and west sea rime on in her head
For ever instead.

Index to First Lines

Notes on Illustrations